W9-CFQ-545

11/13      **DATE DUE**

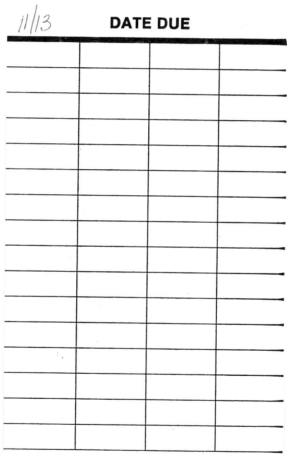

HIGHSMITH 45230

PERSONAL FREEDOM
&
CIVIC DUTY™

UNDERSTANDING
# FREEDOM OF THE PRESS

GINA HAGLER

ROSEN
PUBLISHING®

New York

*To Jason, Seth, and Tess*

Published in 2014 by The Rosen Publishing Group, Inc.
29 East 21st Street, New York, NY 10010

**Library of Congress Cataloging-in-Publication Data**

Hagler, Gina.
Understanding freedom of the press/Gina Hagler.—First edition.
    pages cm.—(Personal freedom & civic duty)
Includes bibliographical references and index.
ISBN 978-1-4488-9465-9 (library binding)
1. Freedom of the press—United States—Juvenile literature. I. Title.
KF4774.H33 2014
342.7308'53—dc23

2012043295

*Manufactured in the United States of America*

CPSIA Compliance Information: Batch #S13YA: For further information, contact Rosen Publishing, New York, New York, at 1-800-237-9932.

# CONTENTS

# INTRODUCTION

The First Amendment of the Constitution guarantees freedom of the press. In fact, it specifically states, "Congress shall make no law respecting an establishment of religion, or prohibiting the free exercise thereof; or abridging the freedom of speech, or the press; or the right to petition the government for a redress of grievances." Sounds simple, but take a closer look: the amendment doesn't spell out exactly what the Founding Fathers intended. The language is broad, and it leaves quite a bit of room for disagreement.

Today people can learn breaking news from sources that range from the Internet to cable news channels.

The idea of a free press was born from the colonists' experiences with British rule. They wanted to be sure their new country would have a press that could report on whatever it wanted, whenever it wanted. They did not want censorship or government oversight of the press.

Today, with online news, blogs, cable news, network news, radio news, and print news, to name a few, we have an abundance of ways for news to be transmitted and received. But is all of this really the news? Are all the ways that people receive their news truly part of a free press? Are blogs and iReports part of what the Framers of the Constitution had in mind?

In the current environment of social media and twenty-four-hour news cycles, it's hard to know if citizens who blog about news events are exercising their rights as journalists. It could be that they're simply exercising their right to free speech. What's the difference?

Our expectations for journalists and newspeople are different than our expectations for people who are voicing their opinion. From journalists, we expect the truth, carefully fact-checked and told in an unbiased way. We expect that journalists will make a distinction between a public figure and a private person when they decide what to write. In short, we expect a level of professionalism and accuracy from a journalist that we don't expect from someone who is tweeting to friends or posting on Facebook.

Today, anything that appears in print or over the airwaves or streaming video is subject to being captured and transmitted via the Internet. Once it's out there, it's available to the public for good. How do we decide what limits to place on journalists and what standards to hold them to?

Here, we'll define freedom of the press and talk about why it was so important to the nation's Founding Fathers. We'll also look at the history of this right and the challenges that have arisen as the presentation of the news has changed. The court cases that helped define the features of a free press will also be examined. Along with this, we'll explore current issues, including the role of a free press in a time of high-speed communication technology. We'll compare the news models of colonial times through the late twentieth century with the wide variety of people and institutions claiming to report the news today, as well as what we can expect the free press to be like in the future.

# WHAT IS FREEDOM OF THE PRESS?

I t has long been said that a free press is essential to democracy. Without a free press, citizens do not have ready access to the information they need to make decisions about issues vital to that democracy. Without that information, they are not truly part of the decision-making process, and the democracy cannot last.

Thomas Jefferson was clearly convinced of this when he wrote a letter to Dr. James Currie in 1786. He wrote, "Our liberty depends on the freedom of the press and that cannot be limited without being lost." George Seldes, a twentieth-century American investigative journalist, was equally convinced of the importance of a free press. He said, "A people that wants to be free must arm itself with a free press."

But what is a free press? How do we know when one exists? Does a free press exist when anyone can print or report anything they wish, without regard for the truth? Does a free press exist when a reporter can present a one-sided argument, leaving out the facts that would give the story balance? Does a free press exist when the norm is reporting a story with only one

President Barack Obama briefs the press on the state of the economy.

source and no opportunity for comment by those named?

Ideally, a free press exists when there is freedom to print anything that is true, without censorship. This freedom from censorship gives the press the opportunity to run stories that are critical of or embarrassing to the government. As long as the information reported is accurate and uncontrolled by government authorities, a free press exists.

But in reality, even a free press is subject to some restrictions: journalists may not be able to share certain information due to government classification. They may not be able to violate a privilege such as the relationship that exists between a lawyer and client or a physician and patient.

Why is a free press important? One could argue

that with so many news outlets, it would be possible for citizens to get the information they need to make important decisions even if the information they received from one source was censored. But think again. If information were censored, with punishment in place for those who did not comply, there would be fewer sources available. With government censorship, the ability to get accurate information would most certainly be compromised.

# FOUNDING FATHERS

During their time as colonists, the Founding Fathers became certain that a free press was essential to their new democracy. They believed it was so important that they wrote it into the Bill of Rights. In understanding why they considered a free press so critical, it's important to remember that many colonists came to this country seeking religious freedom. They wanted to be able to worship as they wished, without any interference from the government. To enjoy this freedom, they left everything behind to come to a new land. Other freedoms were of equal concern to these men, and they fought to ensure them for future generations.

In the broadcast of the television news program *See It Now* on March 9, 1954, noted journalist Edward R. Murrow recognized the courage of the Founding Fathers when he said the following:

*We will not be driven by fear into an age of unreason if we dig deep in our history and our doctrine and remember that we are not descended from fearful men. Not from men who feared to write, to speak, to associate, and to defend the causes that were for the moment unpopular... We can deny our heritage or our history, but we cannot escape responsibility for the results. There is no way for a citizen of a republic to abdicate his responsibilities.*

For Murrow and the journalists who came after him, freedom of the press was not only a liberty guaranteed by the Founding Fathers—it was also a responsibility they would gladly honor.

Not all colonists came to this country for religious freedom. Some came as part of established business ventures. People agreed to come and work for a sponsor until their debt for passage was paid. This benefited colonists who were already in the New World and needed help in their businesses. It also benefited those who wanted to come but had no money to pay their way. Another advantage of this business arrangement was that the British government provided protection and a market for the goods produced by the colonists. The goal was for the colonies and England to have strong economic ties for the good of the British Empire. This worked for a while, but as

Philadelphia, Pennsylvania, is home to life-size bronze statues of Benjamin Franklin and the other Founding Fathers. These thinkers helped establish important guarantees of liberty, including freedom of the press.

time went on and the colonies developed, tensions grew between the colonists and the British government. The British had representatives in the colonies to ensure that the colonists abided by the laws the British put in place. Over time, the colonists became more and more unhappy with the British presence.

At the time, the notion of a free press did not exist. In fact, the concept of a newspaper was just being introduced. In the 1720s, there were three newspapers in the colonies, one each in the major cities of Boston, Philadelphia, and New York. Freedom of the press as an ideal was just around the corner. In 1735, a printer named John Peter Zenger became involved in a legal dispute that would pave the way for a free press. Zenger was the printer for

Libel is an important legal concept in cases involving freedom of the press. Libel is defined as defamation—harming a person's reputation—in writing or in a radio, television, or film broadcast. Defamation can also take place through pictures or other nonverbal means.

To be libelous, the statement or statements must be false. When the statements are about a private citizen, it doesn't matter if the writer meant to cause harm to the person. It is enough that the statements damage the reputation of the person and are false. Minor errors in fact, such as an incorrect address, are not considered libel.

The test of libel is not the same for a public figure—someone who is widely known to the public because he or she is a government official, movie star, business leader, or famous athlete. Simply expressing an unfavorable opinion about a public figure is not libel. There must be malice intended. That is, the person making the statement must be deliberately trying to harm the public figure's reputation with statements he or she knows are untrue or are likely to be untrue.

The current legal interpretation of libel is the result of the U.S. Supreme Court ruling in the *New York Times v. Sullivan* case heard in 1964. In this decision, the Court made a distinction between public figures and private persons, ruling that inaccurate and even defamatory speech is protected under the proper circumstances. The Court decided that in order to protect freedom of the press, people should have a bit more leeway in discussing individuals and matters of great public interest or importance.

New York's first independent political paper, the *New-York Weekly Journal*. Another man, James Alexander, was the founder of the paper and the writer of the pieces that caused the controversy. The pieces Alexander wrote were controversial because they were critical of the newly appointed royal governor, William Cosby. Cosby had used his powers to replace the chief justice of New York after he'd decided a case against Cosby. The governor was not happy with what the *New-York Weekly Journal* had to say about his actions. He issued a proclamation condemning the newspaper's "divers scandalous, virulent, false and seditious reflections." On November 17, 1734, Zenger was arrested and imprisoned for more than eight months before his case went to trial. His trial brought the concept of a free press to the attention of the colonists.

## THE ZENGER TRIAL

The charge brought against Peter Zenger was seditious libel. This charge meant that Zenger was accused of sedition—inciting action against a ruling authority—and libel, or writing something that would hurt a person's reputation. Seditious libel was a legal concept from British common law, under which it was illegal to criticize the royal family or the church. According to British common law at the time of the Zenger trial, it made no difference whether or not the information

The Zenger trial changed the meaning of a charge of libel by considering the truth of disparaging statements for the first time.

printed was true. All that mattered was that the information might harm the reputation of the person discussed. The charges against Zenger were serious despite the fact that his only action was to print content that had been written by someone else. Unfortunately for him, that was all it took to land in trouble.

Andrew Hamilton, an attorney from Philadelphia, represented Zenger at his trial. Hamilton argued that

Zenger could not be guilty of libel because the statements he had printed were true. This was a new interpretation of libel. Up until this point, the truth of a statement had not mattered. It did not protect the person responsible for making the statement. The jury decided the truth did matter and voted to exonerate Zenger, whose wife had continued to print the paper in his absence. The jury's decision changed the definition of libel and established truth as an absolute defense for this crime. It also created the framework for a free press.

Once the concept of the free press was introduced, it became one that the Framers of the Constitution wanted to protect. With this in mind, they included freedom of the press in the Bill of Rights, along with the other rights they deemed essential to a democracy.

## ACCESS TO INFORMATION

To be truly free, the press needs to have unrestricted access to information. In contemporary society, this is not always feasible. Often, organizations or individuals will withhold information until it is to their advantage to release it. It is not illegal for a reporter to write about rumors of a new product launch or a technological innovation that is about to come to market. However, the ability of a reporter to gain this information depends upon his or her sources.

## THE FOURTH ESTATE

It's not uncommon for people to refer to the press as the Fourth Estate. When they do this, they are indicating that they view the press as a group with specific political powers. As you may have guessed, there are three other groups that have been viewed as estates. They have been viewed as estates for far longer than the press has—since the time of feudal society in France and Britain.

The term "estate" refers to a particular class of people. It comes from the Latin term *ad status*, which means "to the estate." It applied to social classes and the occupations of men in the Middle Ages. Each of the estates had defined roles in medieval society. Each performed a specific function.

The First Estate consisted of the church and clergy. The occupation of the men in this estate was to pray and conduct the business of the church. The Second Estate consisted of the nobility and knights. The occupation of the men in this estate was to fight—to protect society from enemies. The Third Estate consisted of everyone else. These were the peasants who grew the food that sustained the people in the other estates. Without all three estates, feudal society would not have functioned smoothly.

After the press was firmly established, it became viewed as the Fourth Estate. The earliest confirmed references to the Fourth Estate date to the mid-1800s.

A source is a person or document that provides information to a reporter. Because sources are vital to reporters in uncovering stories that people or institutions may want to hide, protecting a source's identity is sometimes important. In some cases, reporters have had legal difficulties when sources that gave information anonymously were needed to step forward and verify that the information was accurate.

Another challenge for a free press is the designation of some government information as classified. A reporter following a story about government activities may not experience censorship, but it may not be possible to get the information required because it is not available to reporters or the public. When this occurs and reporters go to sources that "leak" classified information, it can cause a great deal of controversy.

## THE ROLE OF A FREE PRESS

The United States has a free press. Because of this, reporters are free to print truthful reports of government activity. They are free to print truthful reports about public officials and individual citizens. They are free to criticize the government and raise questions about policies and practices that they find questionable. These freedoms are part of the freedom of the press protected by the Bill of Rights and first tested in the Zenger trial.

Even with the guarantee of freedom of the press in the Bill of Rights, there are many questions that arise with regard to the daily details of journalism. For example, there are questions as to who is and who isn't considered a journalist, what protection a journalist can offer a source, and how journalists can use classified information that has been leaked to news organizations or individuals.

Imagine what it was like to envision and plan an entirely new form of government. The Founding Fathers had to decide which rights were essential and needed protection. They had to decide how the voice of the populace would be heard on matters of importance. They had to decide what was required for a person to run for public office. They also

Sometimes reporters who protect their sources become the news. This was the case for former *New York Times* reporter Judith Miller, who went to jail in 2005 after refusing to reveal a confidential source.

had to devise a system of checks and balances that would allow the government to continue for generations to come. The fact that the Framers of the Constitution believed freedom of the press warranted its place in the First Amendment tells us it was vital to the new government they had in mind.

I n the strictest sense, when we speak of the press, we're speaking about newspapers. Newspapers were first introduced in the cities of Europe in the 1600s and 1700s. These early newspapers did not look like the thick publications with multiple sections that we are familiar with today. The earliest weekly newspapers were in the form of Dutch corantos, with two to four pages of news packed tightly, or in the style of the German weeklies. These weeklies were pamphlets of eight to twenty-four pages. Early newspapers were scheduled for publication on a certain day each week. They contained the news of the week and were easy to produce if you had a printing press.

## NEWSPAPERS CHANGE AMERICA

Newspapers came to the American colonies a number of years after they first appeared in Europe. This was due to the fact that, early on, there were no large cities in the colonies to support a newspaper. Also, in the 1600s, the British government kept tight control over the colonies, including the kinds of information published there.

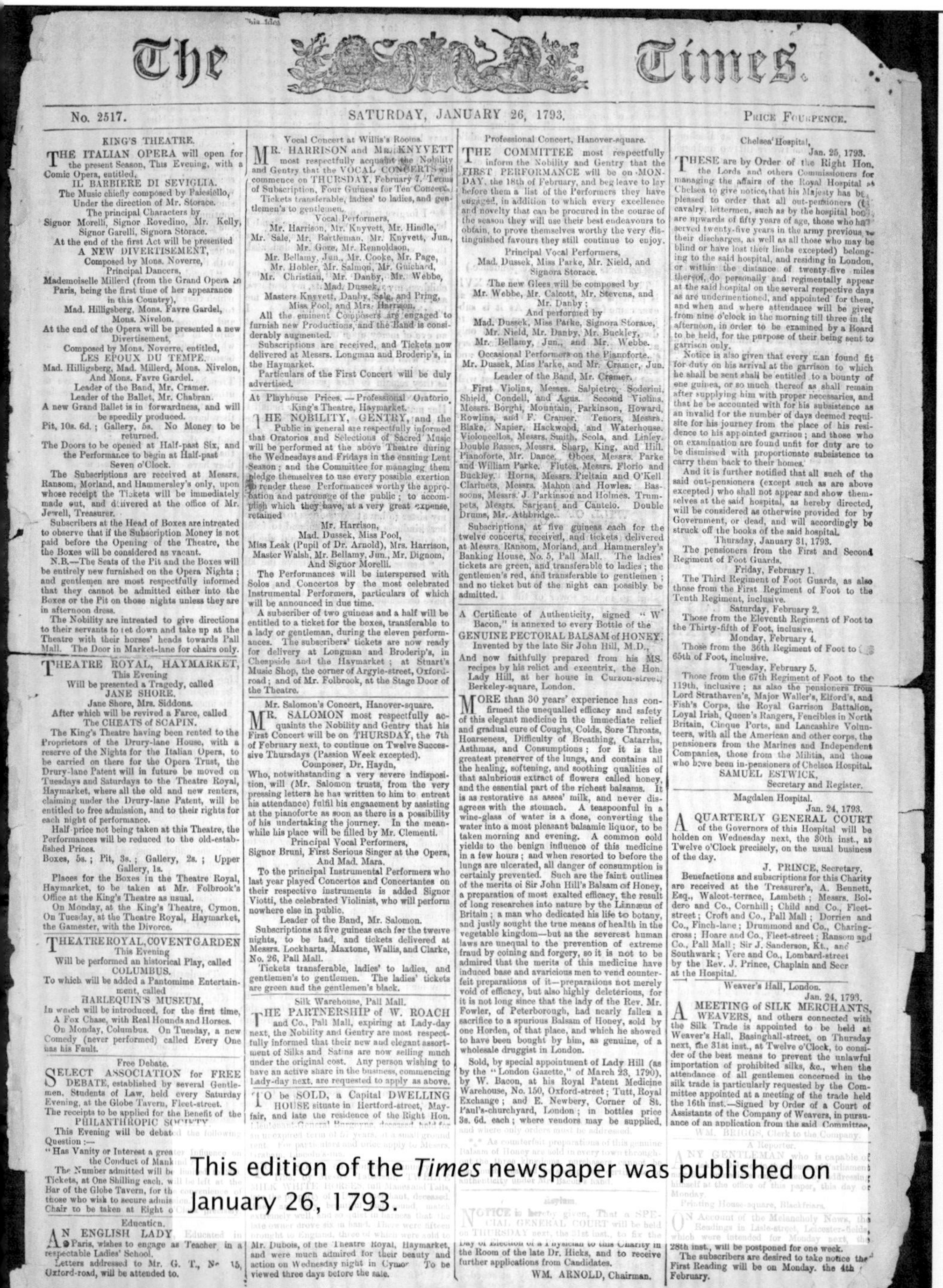

# The Times.

No. 2517. SATURDAY, JANUARY 26, 1793. PRICE FOURPENCE.

KING'S THEATRE.

THE ITALIAN OPERA will open for the present Season, This Evening, with a Comic Opera, entitled,
IL BARBIERE DI SEVIGLIA.
The Music chiefly composed by Paiesiello,
Under the direction of Mr. Storace.
The principal Characters by
Signor Morelli, Signor Rovedino, Mr. Kelly, Signor Garelli, Signora Storace.
At the end of the first Act will be presented
A NEW DIVERTISEMENT,
Composed by Mons. Noverre,
Principal Dancers,
Mademoiselle Millerd (from the Grand Opera in Paris, being the first time of her appearance in this Country),
Mad. Hilligsberg, Mons. Favre Gardel,
Mons. Nivelon.
At the end of the Opera will be presented a new Divertisement,
Composed by Mons. Noverre, entitled,
LES EPOUX DU TEMPE.
Mad. Hilligsberg, Mad. Millerd, Mons. Nivelon,
And Mons. Favre Gardel.
Leader of the Band, Mr. Cramer.
Leader of the Ballet, Mr. Chabran.
A new Grand Ballet is in forwardness, and will be speedily produced.
Pit, 10s. 6d. ; Gallery, 5s. No Money to be returned.
The Doors to be opened at Half-past Six, and the Performance to begin at Half-past Seven o'Clock.

The Subscriptions are received at Messrs. Ransom, Morland, and Hammersley's only, upon whose receipt the Tickets will be immediately made out, and delivered at the office of Mr. Jewell, Treasurer.

Subscribers at the Head of Boxes are intreated to observe that if the Subscription Money is not paid before the Opening of the Theatre, the the Boxes will be considered as vacant.

N.B.—The Seats of the Pit and the Boxes will be entirely new furnished on the Opera Nights ; and gentlemen are most respectfully informed that they cannot be admitted either into the Boxes or the Pit on those nights unless they are in afternoon dress.

The Nobility are intreated to give directions to their servants to set down and take up at the Theatre with their horses' heads towards Pall Mall. The Door in Market-lane for chairs only.

THEATRE ROYAL, HAYMARKET,
This Evening
Will be presented a Tragedy, called
JANE SHORE.
Jane Shore, Mrs. Siddons.
After which will be revived a Farce, called
The CHEATS of SCAPIN.

The King's Theatre having been rented to the Proprietors of the Drury-lane House, with a reserve of the Nights for the Italian Opera, to be carried on there for the Opera Trust, the Drury-lane Patent will in future be moved on Tuesdays and Saturdays to the Theatre Royal, Haymarket, where all the old and new renters, claiming under the Drury-lane Patent, will be entitled to free admission, and to their rights for each night of performance.

Half-price not being taken at this Theatre, the Performances will be reduced to the old-established Prices.
Boxes, 5s. ; Pit, 3s. ; Gallery, 2s. ; Upper Gallery, 1s.

Places for the Boxes in the Theatre Royal, Haymarket, to be taken at Mr. Folbrook's Office at the King's Theatre as usual.

On Monday, at the King's Theatre, Cymon. On Tuesday, at the Theatre Royal, Haymarket, the Gamester, with the Divorce.

THEATRE ROYAL, COVENT GARDEN
This Evening
Will be performed an historical Play, called
COLUMBUS.
To which will be added a Pantomime Entertainment, called
HARLEQUIN'S MUSEUM,
In which will be introduced, for the first time,
A Fox Chase, with Real Hounds and Horses.
On Monday, Columbus. On Tuesday, a new Comedy (never performed) called Every One has his Fault.

Free Debate.

SELECT ASSOCIATION for FREE DEBATE, established by several Gentlemen, Students of Law, held every Saturday Evening, at the Globe Tavern, Fleet-street.
The receipts to be applied for the Benefit of the
PHILANTHROPIC SOCIETY.
This Evening will be debated the following Question :—
"Has Vanity or Interest a greater Influence on the Conduct of Mankind ?"
The Number admitted will be [illegible]
Tickets, at One Shilling each, will be left at the Bar of the Globe Tavern, for the convenience of those who wish to secure admission. Chair to be taken at Eight o'Clock [illegible]

Education.

AN ENGLISH LADY, Educated in Paris, wishes to engage as Teacher in a respectable Ladies' School.
Letters addressed to Mr. G. T., No. 15, Oxford-road, will be attended to.

Vocal Concert at Willis's Rooms.

MR. HARRISON and Mr. KNYVETT most respectfully acquaint the Nobility and Gentry that the VOCAL CONCERTS will commence on THURSDAY, February 7. Terms of Subscription, Four Guineas for Ten Concerts.
Tickets transferable, ladies' to ladies, and gentlemen's to gentlemen.
Vocal Performers,
Mr. Harrison, Mr. Knyvett, Mr. Hindle,
Mr. Sale, Mr. Bartleman, Mr. Knyvett, Jun.,
Mr. Gore, Mr. Rennoldson,
Mr. Bellamy, Jun., Mr. Cooke, Mr. Page,
Mr. Hobler, Mr. Salmon, Mr. Guichard,
Mr. Christian, Mr. Danby, Mr. Webbe,
Mad. Dussek,
Masters Knyvett, Danby, Sale, and Pring,
Miss Pool, and Mrs. Harrison.
All the eminent Composers are engaged to furnish new Productions, and the Band is considerably augmented.
Subscriptions are received, and Tickets now delivered at Messrs. Longman and Broderip's, in the Haymarket.
Particulars of the First Concert will be duly advertised.

At Playhouse Prices.—Professional Oratorio.
King's Theatre, Haymarket.

THE NOBILITY, GENTRY, and the Public in general are respectfully informed that Oratorios and Selections of Sacred Music will be performed at the above Theatre during the Wednesdays and Fridays in the ensuing Lent Season ; and the Committee for managing them pledge themselves to use every possible exertion to render these Performances worthy the approbation and patronage of the public ; to accomplish which they have, at a very great expense, retained
Mr. Harrison,
Mad. Dussek, Miss Pool,
Miss Leak (Pupil of Dr. Arnold), Mrs. Harrison,
Master Walsh, Mr. Bellamy, Jun., Mr. Dignom,
And Signor Morelli.
The Performances will be interspersed with Solos and Concertos by the most celebrated Instrumental Performers, particulars of which will be announced in due time.
A subscriber of two guineas and a half will be entitled to a ticket for the boxes, transferable to a lady or gentleman, during the eleven performances. The subscribers' tickets are now ready for delivery at Longman and Broderip's, in Cheapside and the Haymarket ; at Stuart's Music Shop, the corner of Argyle-street, Oxford-road ; and of Mr. Folbrook, at the Stage Door of the Theatre.

Mr. Salomon's Concert, Hanover-square.

MR. SALOMON most respectfully acquaints the Nobility and Gentry that his First Concert will be on THURSDAY, the 7th of February next, to continue on Twelve Successive Thursdays (Passion Week excepted).
Composer, Dr. Haydn,
Who, notwithstanding a very severe indisposition, will (Mr. Salomon trusts, from the very pressing letters he has written to him to entreat his attendance) fulfil his engagement by assisting at the pianoforte as soon as there is a possibility of his undertaking the journey. In the meanwhile his place will be filled by Mr. Clementi.
Principal Vocal Performers,
Signor Bruni, First Serious Singer at the Opera,
And Mad. Mara.
To the principal Instrumental Performers who last year played Concertos and Concertantes on their respective instruments is added Signor Viotti, the celebrated Violinist, who will perform nowhere else in public.
Leader of the Band, Mr. Salomon.
Subscriptions at five guineas each for the twelve nights, to be had, and tickets delivered at Messrs. Lockharts, Maxtone, Wallis, and Clarke, No. 26, Pall Mall.
Tickets transferable, ladies' to ladies, and gentlemen's to gentlemen. The ladies' tickets are green and the gentlemen's black.

Silk Warehouse, Pall Mall.

THE PARTNERSHIP of W. ROACH and Co., Pall Mall, expiring at Lady-day next, the Nobility and Gentry are most respectfully informed that their new and elegant assortment of Silks and Satins are now selling much under the original cost. Any person wishing to have an active share in the business, commencing Lady-day next, are requested to apply as above.

TO be SOLD, a Capital DWELLING HOUSE situate in Hertford-street, May-fair, and late the residence of the Right Hon. Lieutenant-General Burgoyne, deceased, held for an unexpired term of [illegible] years, at a small ground rent. For particulars and price apply to Messrs. [illegible]

[illegible] SILK WHITE HORSES, full Manes and Tails, late the property of [illegible], deceased. [illegible] beautiful and sound, match extremely well, and so quiet in harness that the late owner drove six in hand. There were fifteen brought to England, three of which were sold to Mr. Dubois, of the Theatre Royal, Haymarket, and were much admired for their beauty and action on Wednesday night in Cymon. To be viewed three days before the sale.

Professional Concert, Hanover-square.

THE COMMITTEE most respectfully inform the Nobility and Gentry that the FIRST PERFORMANCE will be on MONDAY, the 18th of February, and beg leave to lay before them a list of the Performers they have engaged, in addition to which every excellence and novelty that can be procured in the course of the season they will use their best endeavours to obtain, to prove themselves worthy the very distinguished favours they still continue to enjoy.
Principal Vocal Performers,
Mad. Dussek, Miss Parke, Mr. Nield, and Signora Storace.
The new Glees will be composed by
Mr. Webbe, Mr. Calcott, Mr. Stevens, and Mr. Danby ;
And performed by
Mad. Dussek, Miss Parke, Signora Storace,
Mr. Nield, Mr. Danby, Mr. Buckley,
Mr. Bellamy, Jun., and Mr. Webbe.
Occasional Performers on the Pianoforte.
Mr. Dussek, Miss Parke, and Mr. Cramer, Jun.
Leader of the Band, Mr. Cramer.
First Violins, Messrs. Salpietro, Soderini, Shield, Condell, and Agus. Second Violins, Messrs. Borghi, Mountain, Parkinson, Howard, Rowlins, and F. Cramer. Tenors, Messrs. Blake, Napier, Hackwood, and Waterhouse. Violoncellos, Messrs. Smith, Scola, and Linley. Double Basses, Messrs. Sharp, King, and Hill. Pianoforte, Mr. Dance. Oboes, Messrs. Parke and William Parke. Flutes, Messrs. Florio and Buckley. Horns, Messrs. Pieltain and O'Kell. Clarinets, Messrs. Mahon and Howles. Bassoons, Messrs. J. Parkinson and Holmes. Trumpets, Messrs. Sarjeant and Cantelo. Double Drums, Mr. Athbridge.
Subscriptions, at five guineas each for the twelve concerts, received, and tickets delivered at Messrs. Ransom, Morland, and Hammersley's Banking House, No. 5, Pall Mall. The ladies' tickets are green, and transferable to ladies ; the gentlemen's red, and transferable to gentlemen ; and no ticket but of the night can possibly be admitted.

A Certificate of Authenticity, signed "W Bacon," is annexed to every Bottle of the
GENUINE PECTORAL BALSAM of HONEY,
Invented by the late Sir John Hill, M.D.,
And now faithfully prepared from his MS. recipes by his relict and executrix, the Hon. Lady Hill, at her house in Curzon-street, Berkeley-square, London.

MORE than 30 years' experience has confirmed the unequalled efficacy and safety of this elegant medicine in the immediate relief and gradual cure of Coughs, Colds, Sore Throats, Hoarseness, Difficulty of Breathing, Catarrhs, Asthmas, and Consumptions ; for it is the greatest preserver of the lungs, and contains all the healing, softening, and soothing qualities of that salubrious extract of flowers called honey, and the essential part of the richest balsams. It is as restorative as asses' milk, and never disagrees with the stomach. A teaspoonful in a wine-glass of water is a dose, converting the water into a most pleasant balsamic liquor, to be taken morning and evening. A common cold yields to the benign influence of this medicine in a few hours ; and when resorted to before the lungs are ulcerated, all danger of consumption is certainly prevented. Such are the faint outlines of the merits of Sir John Hill's Balsam of Honey, a preparation of most exalted efficacy, the result of long researches into nature by the Linnæus of Britain ; a man who dedicated his life to botany, and justly sought the true means of health in the vegetable kingdom—but as the severest human laws are unequal to the prevention of extreme fraud by coining and forgery, so it is not to be admired that the merits of this medicine have induced base and avaricious men to vend counterfeit preparations of it—preparations not merely void of efficacy, but also highly deleterious, for it is not long since that the lady of the Rev. Mr. Fowler, of Peterborough, had nearly fallen a sacrifice to a spurious Balsam of Honey, sold by one Horden, of that place, and which he showed to have been bought by him, as genuine, of a wholesale druggist in London.

Sold, by special appointment of Lady Hill (as by the "London Gazette," of March 23, 1790), by W. Bacon, at his Royal Patent Medicine Warehouse, No. 150, Oxford-street ; Tutt, Royal Exchange ; and E. Newbery, Corner of St. Paul's-churchyard, London ; in bottles price 3s. 6d. each ; where vendors may be supplied, and where only orders must be addressed.

*** As counterfeit preparations of this genuine Balsam of Honey are sold in every town throughout the three kingdoms, purchasers cannot be [illegible] authenticity under Mr. Bacon's hand.

Asylum.

NOTICE is hereby given, That a SPECIAL GENERAL COURT will be held on THURSDAY next, the 31st inst., to fix the Day of Election of a Physician to this Charity in the Room of the late Dr. Hicks, and to receive further applications from Candidates.
WM. ARNOLD, Chairman.

Chelsea Hospital,
Jan. 25, 1793.

THESE are by Order of the Right Hon. the Lords and others Commissioners for managing the affairs of the Royal Hospital at Chelsea to give notice, that his Majesty has been pleased to order that all out-pensioners (the cavalry, lettermen, such as by the hospital books are upwards of fifty years of age, those who have served twenty-five years in the army previous to their discharges, as well as all those who may be blind or have lost their limbs excepted) belonging to the said hospital, and residing in London, or within the distance of twenty-five miles thereof, do personally and regimentally appear at the said hospital on the several respective days as are undermentioned, and appointed for them, and when and where attendance will be given from nine o'clock in the morning till three in the afternoon, in order to be examined by a Board to be held, for the purpose of their being sent to garrison only.

Notice is also given that every man found fit for duty on his arrival at the garrison to which he shall be sent shall be entitled to a bounty of one guinea, or so much thereof as shall remain after supplying him with proper necessaries, and that he be accounted with for his subsistence as an invalid for the number of days deemed requisite for his journey from the place of his residence to his appointed garrison ; and those who on examination are found unfit for duty are to be dismissed with proportionate subsistence to carry them back to their homes.

And it is further notified that all such of the said out-pensioners (except such as are above excepted) who shall not appear and show themselves at the said hospital, as hereby directed, will be considered as otherwise provided for by Government, or dead, and will accordingly be struck off the books of the said hospital.

Thursday, January 31, 1793.
The pensioners from the First and Second Regiment of Foot Guards.
Friday, February 1.
The Third Regiment of Foot Guards, as also those from the First Regiment of Foot to the Tenth Regiment, inclusive.
Saturday, February 2.
Those from the Eleventh Regiment of Foot to the Thirty-fifth of Foot, inclusive.
Monday, February 4.
Those from the 36th Regiment of Foot to [illegible] 65th of Foot, inclusive.
Tuesday, February 5.
Those from the 67th Regiment of Foot to the 119th, inclusive ; as also the pensioners from Lord Strathaven's, Major Waller's, Elford's, and Fish's Corps, the Royal Garrison Battalion, Loyal Irish, Queen's Rangers, Fencibles in North Britain, Cinque Ports, and Lancashire Volunteers, with all the American and other corps, the pensioners from the Marines and Independent Companies, those from the Militia, and those who have been in-pensioners of Chelsea Hospital.
SAMUEL ESTWICK,
Secretary and Register.

Magdalen Hospital.
Jan. 24, 1793.

A QUARTERLY GENERAL COURT of the Governors of this Hospital will be holden on Wednesday next, the 30th inst., at Twelve o'Clock precisely, on the usual business of the day.
J. PRINCE, Secretary.
Benefactions and subscriptions for this Charity are received at the Treasurer's, A. Bennett, Esq., Walcot-terrace, Lambeth ; Messrs. Boldero and Co., Cornhill ; Child and Co., Fleet-street ; Croft and Co., Pall Mall ; Dorrien and Co., Finch-lane ; Drummond and Co., Charing-cross ; Hoare and Co., Fleet-street ; Ransom and Co., Pall Mall ; Sir J. Sanderson, Kt., and Southwark ; Vere and Co., Lombard-street by the Rev. J. Prince, Chaplain and Secr at the Hospital.

Weaver's Hall, London.
Jan. 24, 1793.

A MEETING of SILK MERCHANTS, WEAVERS, and others connected with the Silk Trade is appointed to be held at Weaver's Hall, Basinghall-street, on Thursday next, the 31st inst., at Twelve o'Clock, to consider of the best means to prevent the unlawful importation of prohibited silks, &c., when the attendance of all gentlemen concerned in the silk trade is particularly requested by the Committee appointed at a meeting of the trade held the 16th inst.—Signed by Order of a Court of Assistants of the Company of Weavers, in pursuance of an application from the said Committee,
WM. BRIGGS, Clerk to the Company.

A Reporter.

ANY GENTLEMAN who is capable of [illegible] Parliament [illegible] addressing himself at the office of this paper, this day or Monday.
Printing House-square, Blackfriars.

ON Account of the Melancholy News, the Readings in Lisle-street, Leicester-fields, which were intended for Monday next, the 28th inst., will be postponed for one week.
The subscribers are desired to take notice the First Reading will be on Monday. the 4th February.

This edition of the *Times* newspaper was published on January 26, 1793.

As a result, a regular news publication was a revolutionary concept in America in the 1700s. For the first time, people who could read were able to learn about events that had occurred beyond their immediate circle of acquaintances. Everyone who read about a newsworthy event would also learn the same facts, without those facts being altered by repeated telling.

The regular publication of newspapers allowed the colonists to receive much more news than before. Also, the fact that information was captured for all to read gave an air of authenticity to the news that had not existed when it was passed from person to person through retelling. With print, news changed from intelligent gossip into something that was believed to be more reliable. In addition, newspapers began to include advertisements, shipping schedules, and other pieces of information that were soon seen as essential. Newspapers quickly became an important part of commerce in their cities of publication.

Once newspapers became an accepted source of news and weeklies became dailies, their coverage spread into new areas, including advice, recipes, and properties for sale. Special editions were published when breaking news occurred. People learned to depend upon newspapers as a source of content related to their daily lives and business interests. Because newspapers were considered reliable, people believed what they read.

# FROM PRINT TO THE AIRWAVES

The role of newspapers in the United States was firmly established when magazines entered the arena. The first truly successful magazine in the United States was the *Saturday Evening Post*. First published in 1821, it covered general-interest topics like entertainment and included short stories and cover artwork by Norman Rockwell. *Time* magazine, first published in November 1936, was a news magazine from the start. The difference between a magazine such as *Time* and a daily or weekly newspaper was that *Time* could select a topic and look at it in depth. *Time* was not trying to bring breaking news to the public. It was putting the news in context, bringing a deeper meaning to events than a newspaper story—designed to present the facts in the most direct way possible—ever could.

Meanwhile, technological advancement led to the development of the radio. People could hear the news on the radio. They did not need to read it. The top stories were easy to identify and follow. The first radio news broadcast was made over station 8MK in Detroit, Michigan, on August 31, 1920. Sports broadcasts began in 1921 with coverage of a college football game between West Virginia and Pittsburgh. With radio broadcasts, it was possible to report on an event in progress, like a sporting event. It was also

The Saturday Evening
POST
October 5, 1957 — 15¢

I CALL ON
CLARK GABLE
By PETE MARTIN

Japan vs. Girard: The Inside Sto

General-interest magazines like the *Saturday Evening Post* have been popular sources of information since the 1800s. This issue, with cover art by Dick Sargent, was published in 1957.

DICK SARGENT

Students listen to a lesson in current events that is being broadcast over the radio in 1926.

possible to report on events that happened after the printing and distribution of the newspaper each day.

Eventually, all-news stations dedicated their programming time to reporting on news, sports, weather, and traffic. Up-to-the-minute radio news meant that people could make decisions based on what was happening at that moment. Radio news possessed an immediacy that newspapers and news magazines could not hope to match.

## TELEVISION ARRIVES

Televised news programs were the next innovation. People had been experimenting with television since the late 1920s, but it wasn't until November 2, 1936, that the BBC in Britain transmitted the world's first regular

A New York family gathers around the television in 1950. Television has been informing and entertaining American families since the mid-twentieth century.

television news broadcast as we know it today. In the United States, people knew about television because it had been demonstrated at the 1939 World's Fair. The first-ever television news broadcast in America was in 1930, and the first regularly scheduled television news broadcast was in 1940. But television did not become part of mainstream American life until after World War II ended in 1945.

Once television became part of American life, televised news broadcasts occurred as regularly scheduled

## POLITICAL IMPACT OF TELEVISION NEWS

During the Cold War that began after World War II ended, Senator Joseph McCarthy called individuals before the House Un-American Activities Committee to investigate them for alleged involvement in subversive activities and having Communist ties. There was little or no proof of such ties, but those called before the committee often had their careers and lives ruined.

Edward R. Murrow, vice president of CBS and moderator of *See It Now*, aired a broadcast on March 9, 1954, that was critical of McCarthy's methods. During this weekly news show, Murrow said, "The line between investigating and persecuting is a very fine one...We must remember always that accusation is not proof and that conviction depends upon evidence and due process of law."

Murrow offered McCarthy an opportunity to present his views on a future program. McCarthy chose to film his response, in which he referred to Murrow as "the cleverest of the jackal pack" that attacked when Communists were being identified. McCarthy also said the reaction against his work grew in intensity with its success. "In conclusion," McCarthy said, "may I say that under the shadow of the most horrible and destructive weapons that man has ever devised we fight to save our country, our homes, our children. To this cause, ladies and gentlemen, I have dedicated and will continue to dedicate all that I have and all that I am."

The result of this broadcast was the eventual discrediting of McCarthy's methods and the end of the hearings. It was the first time that a television news broadcast had such a huge political impact.

programs. They were generally timed for early evening, after the workday was complete, and late evening, when most adults would be finishing up the day and heading to bed. The anchors on these news shows were trusted and respected professionals. Weekly news programs like Murrow's *See It Now* were also broadcast. Vital breaking news, such as the assassination of President John F. Kennedy in 1963, was reported immediately, interrupting regularly scheduled programming.

With the passage of the 1984 Cable Act, cable television quickly gained viewers in the United States. By the early 1990s, nearly fifty-three million households subscribed to cable. On June 1, 1980, the Cable News Network (CNN) launched its first newscast. Cable news became an important part of American life. With cable news, it was possible to have stations dedicated solely to the reporting of news, domestic and international, twenty-four hours a day, seven days a week. It was no longer the case that news programs aired only at set times, with interruptions of other programming for momentous events. Americans could catch up on the news on cable at any time. During broadcasts, a crawler running across the bottom of the television screen would even update other stories while the people on-screen were reporting about something else. With its coverage of the first Persian Gulf War in

1991, CNN established itself as a major player in news reporting.

The Internet and the World Wide Web began to enter American homes in the 1990s. At first, the content consisted mainly of e-mail and informational Web pages with very basic links. On August 30, 1995, CNN launched an Internet news site. Soon anyone at a computer had access to the latest news from CNN .com and the many other dedicated news sites that followed. By 2008, CNN was offering live broadcasts over the Internet. Now people could have the same news experience as on television while nowhere near a television set.

## OTHER FORMS OF NEWS

By the mid-1990s, individuals were posting story links and distributing content on the Internet. One of the earliest distributors of news was Matt Drudge of *The Drudge Report*. His Web site, DrudgeReport.com, which began as an e-mail newsletter, linked to stories from many different news sites. Drudge has also broken several large stories, such as the Bill Clinton—Monica Lewinsky scandal in 1998. However, he has been questioned about the originality of a number of stories that he has claimed to be exclusive. Some of his facts have also been called into question. For example, in 2004, Drudge apologized after incorrectly reporting

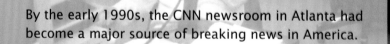

By the early 1990s, the CNN newsroom in Atlanta had become a major source of breaking news in America.

that presidential candidate John Kerry had an affair with an intern. The question of whether or not individuals like Drudge, who work independently to bring news to people, are considered part of a free press has also been hotly debated. However, despite the controversy, Drudge's Web site continues to be an important and popular source of news, getting millions of hits per day.

Blogs and social media are two other forms of news distribution that have caused people to examine what it means to be part of a free press. Are blog posts and tweets considered speech or the press? Is someone who blogs the news held to the same standards as someone working for the *New York Times* or CNN? These are just a few of the controversies that have arisen with the

Tweeters and bloggers send out news from NASA's Jet Propulsion Laboratory after the Mars rover *Curiosity* successfully landed on Mars on August 5, 2012. The Twitter hashtag #CONGRATS is written in peanuts on their desk.

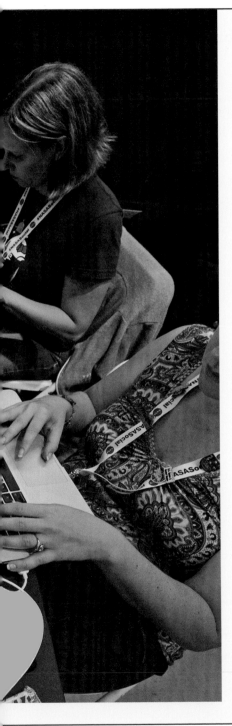

availability of technology and the ability to broadcast news from a wide variety of platforms.

The fact is, all of the types of media mentioned are part of our news sources today. From conventional to electronic newspapers, news magazines, radio, cable, the Internet, and social media like Twitter and Facebook, there are more ways to get news today than at any other time in history. Each news outlet must find and cultivate sources for the information needed.

Today, the free press does not only refer to newspapers. The protections and responsibilities of a free press apply to other sources of news as well. No matter how they are distributing the information, reporters must report the news in a timely way while keeping their readers' respect by being accurate and truthful.

As technology evolves, our news will come to us in ways that we cannot imagine now. Journalists will use new and innovative methods. However, a responsible press will still have to meet the requirements of the law as decided in the courts. In fact, many of the specific rights and responsibilities of a free press have been determined through landmark Supreme Court cases.

The Bill of Rights guarantees freedom of the press, but it doesn't say exactly what that means. As a result, our definition of a free press has arisen from the standard practices of journalism and from rulings made by the courts when there has been disagreement. Some cases argued before the U.S. Supreme Court have been so important that the decisions in those cases set precedents for all others involving freedom of the press.

Because the Supreme Court is the highest court in the United States, the decisions that it makes are final. As a result, cases decided by the Supreme Court have a great impact on the laws and society of the United States.

During the second half of the twentieth century, the Supreme Court heard the following landmark cases. The decisions in these cases have helped define the way a free press functions in a variety of circumstances. When new cases involving freedom of the press are heard before the Supreme Court, they are decided using these cases as starting points.

# NEW YORK TIMES CO. V. SULLIVAN

One of the most important Supreme Court cases to expand freedom of the press was *New York Times Co. v. Sullivan* (1964). A group supporting Martin Luther King Jr. had run an advertisement in the *New York Times*. The advertisement contained some incorrect information about civil rights violations against King and other blacks. The city commissioner who oversaw the police department, L. B. Sullivan, sued the *New York Times* for printing untruths about the police of Montgomery, Alabama. Sullivan said that since he was in charge of the police force, the untrue comments had been made about him and had harmed him and his reputation. The state courts in Alabama agreed with Sullivan and ruled in his favor. The *New York Times* appealed the decision to the Supreme Court.

The Supreme Court ruled that freedom of speech protects citizens' right to criticize the government. It further ruled that as long as the untrue statements were not made purposely and with the intention of causing harm—known as actual malice—there was no libel when writing about a public official. As a result of this ruling, members of the news media have been freer to report stories about public matters without fearing that lawsuits will be filed against them.

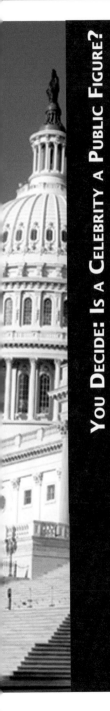

The rules of libel differ for public figures and private persons. For a public figure to be libeled, there must not only be false statements published, but also malice—the intention to do serious harm. Because of this, it makes a difference whether or not someone is considered a public figure or a private person. Government leaders, including politicians, are public figures. So are the heads of large corporations. What about celebrities?

Celebrities are individuals who are familiar to many and are of great public interest. Many celebrities make their living precisely because they are so well known and of such interest to the public. Does that make them public figures in the same sense as politicians?

What if the celebrity is taking a child to school or vacationing with family in a remote location? Are those actions by the celebrity part of his or her role as a public figure? Is there any time when a celebrity is not acting as a public figure?

Actor Tom Cruise has been the target of what he claimed were libelous statements from a number of publications. His lawyer, Bertram Fields, announced a lawsuit against the *National Enquirer* over its coverage of his divorce from actress Katie Holmes. As of September 2012, the case had not been decided, but it is likely to be an important one in defining libel when the subject of the reports is a celebrity.

Members of the Newspaper Guild of New York protest in support of reporters who faced jail time for refusing to reveal their sources.

# BRANZBURG V. HAYES

Paul Branzburg was a newspaper reporter from Kentucky. He had written several articles about illegal drug activity. While gathering research for those articles, he had observed individuals involved in unlawful activity. As a result, he was called on two occasions to appear before a grand jury and testify about the individuals he had observed. Branzburg refused, citing the First Amendment as one source for his protection.

In 1972, the Supreme Court ruled that Branzburg and other reporters in his situation must testify before grand juries because all citizens are responsible for giving testimony in federal criminal cases. Reporters were obligated to disclose confidential information about a crime as long as the information was relevant to an important government interest, such as national security, and the government had no other way to obtain the information. The Court did state that the grand jury had to be conducting its investigation in good faith and could not question a reporter simply to harass him or her. In the opinion and concurring opinion, the justices said they believed that having to testify before a grand jury would not greatly harm a reporter's ability to gather information.

Several other justices wrote dissenting opinions. They asserted that having to testify before a grand jury would most certainly hurt reporters' ability to gather information from sources, since informants would be less likely to speak freely with them. This would result in less information being available to the public.

In this case, the Supreme Court determined that there is no absolute First Amendment protection for those gathering news. As a result of the case, several states passed shield laws to help protect the confidentiality of news sources at the state and local level.

# MIAMI HERALD PUBLISHING CO., DIVISION OF KNIGHT NEWSPAPERS, INC. V. TORNILLO

A political candidate in Florida, Pat Tornillo, brought a lawsuit against the *Miami Herald* after it refused to

The U.S. Supreme Court ruled in favor of the Miami Herald Publishing Company in the case pursued by political candidate Pat Tornillo. The Court declared Florida's right of reply law unconstitutional because it violated the freedom of the press.

print his replies to editorials that were critical of his candidacy. He brought the suit based on Florida's "right of reply" law, which said a candidate had a right to space in a newspaper to reply to criticism and attacks by the paper. The Florida Supreme Court ruled that because there were other methods available to the candidate to express his position, he was not entitled to space in the *Miami Herald* for his replies. Tornillo disagreed, and the Supreme Court heard the case.

The Supreme Court is the highest court in the United States and the final court of appeal. The U.S. Constitution described the Court in general terms. A passage stated that judicial power was to be "vested in one supreme Court, and in such inferior Courts as the Congress may from time to time ordain and establish." The Judiciary Act of 1789 established a three-part judiciary made up of district courts, circuit courts, and the Supreme Court.

Cases come before the Supreme Court in one of two ways. The first is under original jurisdiction. Cases that fall into this category are those involving ambassadors and other diplomats, or cases in which the parties are states. The second way that cases come before the Supreme Court is when there is an appeal of a decision made by a state or federal court in matters involving constitutional issues.

The Supreme Court does not hear every eligible case. In fact, the justices hear only seventy-five to eighty cases out of the ten thousand petitions they receive annually.

To be heard before the Supreme Court, the losing party in a lower court must file a writ of certiorari. The writ includes a statement of the facts of the case, the legal questions needing review, and the arguments in favor of the Court granting the writ. Four justices must agree that a case should be heard. Their decision is based upon such criteria as whether or not the case includes questions of federal law or of the Constitution. If the justices decline to hear the case, the ruling of the lower court is final. If the justices accept a case and grant the writ, both parties then file briefs outlining the merits of their cases.

At the hearing, the attorney for each party is given the opportunity to make an oral argument of the principles of the case before the justices. At the end of the oral arguments, the case is submitted for a decision. A majority vote of the nine justices decides the case.

Once the case is decided, the most senior justice in the majority assigns another justice in the majority to prepare a draft of the Court's opinion. Justices review the drafts of the opinion, which detail the reasoning of the justices, along with any concurring or dissenting opinions, until the decision is announced. Opinions for all cases are available to the public.

In 1974, the Court ruled unanimously that equal space for rebuttal is not guaranteed under the First Amendment. It struck down Florida's right of reply law as unconstitutional. While it agreed with Tornillo that there was often a monopoly on news distribution in an area—with one company owning the television, radio, and newspaper in a certain location, for example—there were other ways for Tornillo and other candidates to express their opinions. Telling the editors of a newspaper what they must print would be too restrictive of freedom of the press, the justices concluded. As a result, political candidates are not entitled to equal space in a newspaper under the First Amendment.

State official James Tilton *(center)* leads journalists on a tour of a California prison. Journalists may visit prisons and speak with random inmates, but they do not have the right to interview specific prisoners.

# PELL V. PROCUNIER

Several reporters, including Eve Pell, requested permission to question specific California prison inmates. Raymond K. Procunier, director of the California Department of Corrections, refused to grant permission. He said that interviewing individual inmates in the past had led to those inmates being widely known in the prison and having excessive influence over the other inmates, resulting in severe disciplinary problems. He said that individual interviews worked against the purpose of the penal system, but that reporters could visit the prisons and interview prisoners at random. The inmates and Pell claimed that the policy violated the inmates' right to free speech. They also claimed that a free press must have access to individual prisoners in order for the press to report on prison conditions accurately.

The Supreme Court ruled in 1974 that as long as reporters could visit the prison and interview random prisoners, they had the ability to report on prison conditions. The majority opinion stated that the press had the same access to prisoners as the general public and that was enough to serve the purposes of the First Amendment.

Several justices expressed their disagreement. They wrote that the prisoners' First Amendment right to free speech entitled them to give interviews. They also wrote that the prison could carry out its duties even if the press had access to specific inmates.

As a result of this case, reporters do not have the right to conduct face-to-face interviews with specific inmates. They also do not have the right to prison access that is greater than that of the general public.

# NEBRASKA PRESS ASSOCIATION V. STUART

A Nebraska state trial judge, Hugh Stuart, had a murder case on his docket. The facts of the case were shocking, and he expected the case to attract a great deal of attention from the news media. In an effort to protect the accused's Sixth Amendment rights, Stuart issued a gag order on the press so that there could be no reporting of evidence revealed in the pretrial phase. The judge's intention was to prevent potential jury members from forming an opinion that would make it impossible for the accused to receive a fair trial. The Nebraska Press Association argued that the First Amendment ensured the right of the press to publish information about pretrial proceedings in a case. The lower court found against the Nebraska Press Association. The association appealed to the Supreme Court.

After reviewing the case, the Supreme Court ruled in 1976 that there were other methods for ensuring a fair trial for the accused, even in a sensational trial such as this one. The justices wrote that the press was free to write about what occurred in a courtroom at the pretrial stage. Ordering the press to refrain from publishing anything that would be "strongly implicative" of the defendant was too broad because there was no way to know what exact information would hurt the defendant.

The result was that the press could publish any trial-related information that was legally obtained. Another result was that judges began to make greater use of restraining orders on people participating in pretrial activities. The restraining orders were intended to prevent participants from making statements that would incite public opinion against the accused before the trial began.

# ZURCHER V. STANFORD DAILY

The *Stanford Daily* newspaper published a story about a violent confrontation between police and demonstrators at Stanford University's hospital. Afterward, the police used a warrant to search the newsroom for negatives and photographs that would identify the demonstrators involved. *The Daily* argued that since the staff was not involved in any unlawful action, the newsroom should not be subject to a search. The paper argued that such a search violated the First Amendment and two other amendments. It also argued that police searches of newsrooms would severely harm journalists' ability to gather and publish the news. In addition to disrupting the publication process, newsroom searches would intimidate staff and decrease the number of confidential sources willing to talk to reporters.

The police argued that it made no difference that the newspeople were not involved in the crime. It only mattered that there was probable cause that evidence of the crime existed at that location.

The Supreme Court ruled in 1978 that the conditions and steps necessary to obtain a search warrant were sufficient to protect the rights of the newspaper. Therefore, it was constitutional for a search warrant to be used to search a newsroom. However, the Court said that the search warrant should be very specific as to what evidence was being sought. The dissenting justices argued that search warrants should only be used when there was reason to believe that issuing a subpoena for the newspaper to turn over specific materials would result in those materials being destroyed.

After the Court's ruling in favor of the search warrants, a huge amount of criticism of the ruling appeared in the press. As a result, Congress passed the Privacy Protection Act of 1980. Under this act, the government cannot search press offices unless there is reason to believe that the reporter or paper is involved in the crime or that the evidence will be destroyed if a subpoena is served. As a result of this legislation, police in most cases must issue a subpoena for information that they seek from a newsroom. They must give the newsroom time to turn over the specific materials requested instead of using a warrant to search the newsroom itself.

# WHAT THESE LANDMARK CASES MEAN TO FREEDOM OF THE PRESS

The rulings in these landmark cases elaborated the meaning of freedom of the press. As a result of these and other decisions, there are different rules as to

A newsroom is the place where journalists prepare their stories and meet with their editors. The Privacy Protection Act of 1980 limits the circumstances under which a newsroom may be searched for evidence of a crime.

what can be printed about a private individual and a public figure. Also as a result of these rulings, a journalist reporting on criminal activity can be called to

testify before a federal grand jury. Equal newspaper space for a political candidate is not ensured under the First Amendment, and reporters are not entitled to any greater access to prison inmates than the general public. Reporting on pretrial proceedings is protected as long as the information is obtained legally.

The Founding Fathers probably could not have envisioned these exact challenges to the First Amendment, but by calling for "one supreme court" to oversee all others, they provided a means for testing the free press provision of the First Amendment. Because of their foresight, the rulings of the Supreme Court have been integral in defining the meaning of a free press.

# CONTEMPORARY CONTROVERSIES

## CHAPTER 4

Two people often view the same event and interpret it differently. Many times, the difference is due to the experience and expectations that each individual brings to the situation. For instance, someone who has had a bad experience with a dog might view a dog's behavior as menacing, while someone who has never had that experience might view the same behavior as adorable.

Usually, the differences in people's views are not large enough to create a serious problem, but sometimes a situation is complex and touches on people's emotions in a way that creates a controversy. When that occurs, it can be difficult to find a single solution to the problem that satisfies everyone involved.

In democracies, controversies often arise around citizens' right to know. There are also controversies about the ways the press collects and distributes information to the public. Many conflicts involve freedom of information, or the right of people to access government documents or sources. While journalists and citizens seek as many details as possible, the government may want to keep some information secret to protect national security or avoid embarrassment. Conflicts like these raise many questions. For example, if there is a leak of intelligence or other classified information, do reporters have the right to report on that information?

Questions also arise from the great changes taking place in technology. What can be done with the information that individuals publish via social media? Can regular citizens act as reporters? Where does free speech end, and a free press begin?

# FREEDOM OF INFORMATION

The Founding Fathers worked to ensure freedom of the press because they were certain that uninformed citizens would be unable to make good decisions about their democracy. Freedom of information is essential to a free press. It does no one any good when a reporter is unable to fully investigate a newsworthy event. Or does it?

When journalists or private individuals need access to information that is held by a government agency, they have a right to that information. In 1966, the Freedom of Information Act (FOIA) was enacted to ensure individual access to information held by government agencies. This right is enforceable in court and applies to all records or parts of records that do not have special protection.

Sometimes sensitive government information is released with parts redacted, or blocked out. Before releasing this 2005 photo, the Pentagon concealed the identities of the servicemen who accompanied this flag-draped casket of a fallen soldier.

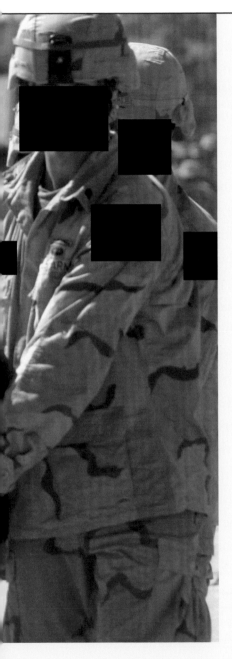

In a video on the FOIA Web site (http://www.foia.gov), Melanie Pustay, director of the Office of Information Policy at the Department of Justice, explains that there are nine categories of exempt information. These include information such as classified documents, personal privacy information, trade secrets, privileged communications, and law enforcement interests. Pustay states, "Now even if an exemption applies, the Attorney General has encouraged all agencies to use their discretion and release information if there's no foreseeable harm in doing so and when disclosure is not otherwise prohibited by law."

If freedom to information is ensured, where is the controversy? A reporter can simply request the necessary information through the

FOIA process. The controversy lies in the interpretation of "foreseeable harm." A reporter following where a story leads her is interested in gathering all the information she can. She may never use the information directly in her story, yet that information may be essential to providing the big picture that she needs to write the piece accurately. The reporter may believe that the information should be provided with the understanding that causing harm is not the intent.

It can be a fine line when the information sought pertains to national security. A government agency might be concerned that releasing information will jeopardize future plans or reveal the identity of important contacts. From the government's perspective, protecting future plans and personnel is essential. From the press perspective, citizens have the right to know about anything the government is doing.

Not all of the information the press seeks is held by government agencies. Sometimes the judicial branch—federal and state courts—may have the information a reporter needs. Or the legislative branch, such as one of the houses of Congress, may hold the information. It's also possible the desired information is held by clandestine government agencies. When the needed information does not fall under the FOIA, members of the press must use other means to push for the information they require. These efforts often create controversy.

# PRESS ACCESS TO GOVERNMENT DOCUMENTS AND OFFICIALS

In the 1980s, the Reagan administration was involved in a foreign policy scandal known as the Iran-Contra affair. During the time of the Iran-Contra affair, there was a difference between the foreign policy that was stated as the official policy and the policy that was actually being conducted. Two government agencies, the National Security Council (NSC) and the Central Intelligence Agency (CIA), were involved.

During the second half of the 1980s, the CIA carried out operations that supported the Contras, rebel groups in Nicaragua, as revealed by the *Wall Street Journal*. These activities took place without the authorization of Congress, even as it worked to close any loopholes that allowed funding to the Contras. In order to bring monetary support to the Contras, Lieutenant Colonel Oliver North, a U.S. Marine who worked on the NSC staff at the White House, hit upon the idea of overcharging Iran for weapons sold to it by the United States. The surplus funds would go to fund the Contra operations, even though the two parties—the Iranians and the Contras—were not connected in any way.

Meanwhile, in Iran, American hostages had been taken. According to an article that appeared in the *New York Times* on July 1, 1985, President Ronald

Reagan stated that the official U.S. policy was the following: "The United States gives terrorists no rewards. We make no concessions, we make no deals." But the United States did sell weapons to Iran, a nation the United States had declared a sponsor of terrorism, in what became known as a "guns-for-hostages" deal. It was never concluded, even after hearings in the matter, what Reagan did and did not know about the affair. But the whole tangled mess was uncovered, and the facts reported were proven to be true.

The Iran-Contra scandal was a major story at the time. News of the story reached the American public via news organizations such as the *Wall Street Journal* and the *New York Times*. Reporters at those papers followed the story even after

Lieutenant-Colonel Oliver North *(left)* was a major participant in the activities that made up the Iran-Contra scandal of the 1980s.

they were misdirected and lied to. Their work resulted in the American public learning of a presidential administration that was deceiving the public.

The controversy lies in the question of whether or not the press should have pursued this story. Was it necessary to expose these activities? Did their reporting hinder the ability of the Reagan administration to carry out its foreign policy? Does it make a difference that the administration's activities were in direct defiance of Congress? Does it matter that the president himself may not have been aware of all the activities that were undertaken? Did the press do the right thing in pushing the story until hearings were held?

History has shown that during this period, illegal activity was taking place at the highest levels of government. The press had discovered a significant story that called the credibility of the president into question. In this instance, the press shone a light on activities that were clearly not being conducted as stated. Without the pressure the press put on the administration, the public might never have learned of these transactions.

## LEAKS OF CLASSIFIED INFORMATION

WikiLeaks has been another source of controversy. The WikiLeaks organization is dedicated to the publication of private, secret, and classified information from anonymous sources, news leaks, and whistle-blowers. Launched in 2006, WikiLeaks states on its Web site that its goal is "to bring important news and information to the public." The site explains:

*We provide an innovative, secure and anonymous way for sources to leak information to our journalists (our electronic drop box). One of our most important activities is to publish original source material alongside our news stories so readers and historians alike can see evidence of the truth.*

A not-for-profit international firm founded by Australian Internet activist Julian Assange, WikiLeaks holds millions of otherwise unavailable documents.

In April 2011, WikiLeaks began to publish secret files related to the prisoners held at the American military detention camp at Guantanamo Bay, Cuba. In all, there were 779 files that were marked "Secret" and "NOFORN" (not releasable to foreign nationals) to indicate that they could not be shared with representatives or citizens of countries other than the United States. The files contained classified assessments of the individuals held, along with interviews and memos. The memos were written internally by the Pentagon's Joint Task Force Guantanamo. None of

Julian Assange of Australia is the founder of WikiLeaks, which is known for publishing secret information.

the information in the files was intended for public viewing.

The *New York Times* published a story based on the information. Although WikiLeaks had shared the documents with other news outlets, the paper insisted it did not receive the documents from WikiLeaks but from another source. The controversy arose over whether or not this sensitive information should have been made public. Some took the view that individual citizens should have the opportunity to assess the danger posed by the detainees, but others argued that the documents were old and were not reliable indicators of the current views of detainees. Another viewpoint was that whether or not the information was new or old, it was secret information and should not have been publicized.

Freedom of information is essential to a free press, yet not all information is readily available. Classified information can be withheld from the public at the discretion of the government. Medical information can be withheld at the discretion of a public official. Tax returns may be requested but may take months to be made public. In reality, the press must act in an environment in which some information will not be made public for decades, if at all.

A reporter's job calls for access to information that is pertinent to the story. Often, especially when first investigating a topic, a reporter may not know the exact information needed because the story has not yet taken shape. For this reason, reporters cast a wide net, interviewing and investigating around the story as events take place.

By working with sources repeatedly and earning their trust, a successful journalist will often be able to get a story first. The journalist may even be able to obtain information that is not available to other reporters. Because of the importance of sources, journalists are careful to keep the identity of their anonymous sources unknown to the public. Yet a journalist cannot print information without checking to be certain it is true. The amount of fact-checking a journalist will do depends on how reliable a source has been in the past and how sensitive the information is. For these reasons, a reporter's relationship with his or her sources is a key part of the day-to-day realities of a free press.

Senators Lindsey Graham and John McCain speak with members of the press at the U.S. Capitol.

WikiLeaks was back in the news in September 2011, when its archive of U.S. State Department diplomatic cables, previously published in redacted form (with key words and names blocked out), appeared on the Internet in their entirety. WikiLeaks had been storing the unredacted cables in an encrypted file. However, the encryption key was published in a book written by reporters David Leigh and Luke Harding, who were employed by former WikiLeaks partner the *Guardian*. WikiLeaks and the *Guardian* argued over who was to blame for letting the file get out and revealing the encryption key.

The controversy in this instance arose because many of the individuals named in the documents were involved in activities that placed their lives in danger if made public. The debate focused on whether or not the availability of these papers was truly necessary. Did the possible usefulness of the information outweigh the danger to the individuals named? Was it up to WikiLeaks to make that decision? Does freedom of the press include the publication of secret or classified information that has been leaked? Supporters of both sides felt very strongly. Some argued that the release and publication of the information was appropriate; others believed these actions crossed a line that should not have been crossed.

# JOURNALISTS AND POLICE HARASSMENT

Another recent conflict revolved around the right of journalists to film police activity occurring in public places. In July 2011, an individual videotaped a police response to criminal activity on Long Island, New York. The person who made the video was Philip Datz, a member of the press in Suffolk County. Datz had press credentials that were plainly visible. He stood on a public sidewalk to film the activity, and he did not interfere with the police while filming. The police officer in charge, Police Sergeant Michael Milton, told Datz to stop filming and leave. When Datz instead moved to a different location, his camera and videotape were forcibly confiscated and he was arrested. He was charged with obstruction of governmental administration, a charge that was later dismissed.

The police in Suffolk County had a history of dispersing people who were filming police activity that was taking place in public view, and Datz filed a lawsuit with the help of the New York Civil Liberties Union and the National Press Photographers Association. The lawsuit claimed that the Suffolk police violated Datz's constitutional rights. According to court documents, Datz's civil rights action challenged "Suffolk County's

Twitter had to hand over the tweets of an Occupy Wall Street protester after this confrontation with police on the Brooklyn Bridge in 2011.

policy, custom, and practice of obstructing the First Amendment right of the press and the public to gather and record news and information about police activity in public places."

Datz hoped the lawsuit would result in the county enacting new policies to protect the First Amendment rights of journalists and citizens. Changes he wanted to see included better training for police officers in dealing with the media and discipline for officers who obstruct journalists from doing their jobs. As of September 2012, the case was still ongoing.

# INDIVIDUALS AND SOCIAL MEDIA

The use of information from social media in criminal trials became a matter of controversy when Judge Matthew

A. Sciarrino Jr. of the New York City Criminal Court in Manhattan ruled that tweets are public comments. The ruling applied to tweets posted by Occupy Wall Street protester Malcolm Harris having to do with his part in a mass march over the Brooklyn Bridge on October 1, 2011. Harris had been arrested after taking part in the march. He had deleted his tweets, but Sciarrino ordered Twitter to turn over the original comments. "If you post a tweet, just like if you scream

A New York City judge ruled that tweets are public, not private, speech.

it out the window, there is no reasonable expectation of privacy," Sciarrino wrote.

Defining tweets as public rather than private speech is an important development for individuals. It also paves the way for reporters to use information from tweets in their reporting.

These are just a few of the controversies that have arisen as new technologies for news reporting have become available. More decisions will have to be made as the ability of non-journalists to publish news content becomes more widely available and accepted.

# A FREE PRESS TODAY AND IN THE FUTURE

## CHAPTER 5

A free press cannot exist without citizens who are dedicated to ensuring its existence. These citizens must not be afraid to go to court to uphold their constitutional right to freedom of the press. They must not be afraid to push for the information and access they need to do their jobs. It helps to be familiar with important Supreme Court cases. It also helps to keep up with news of the latest controversies and legal battles, especially those related to advances in technology and changes in the media. Every new generation takes on new battles in defense of this right.

Not all countries have a free press. In many countries, freedom of the press is not even an ideal, let alone a right. In those countries, the government decides what information is available to the public. In many instances, the government runs the press. It's difficult for us to imagine a press that is overseen by the government. Some say that the press is not truly free in the United States because the government can withhold information it deems too sensitive for publication. But freedom of the press is not an absolute. It is a balance between the need for information on the one hand and the need for government to function on the other.

## ORGANIZATIONS THAT PROTECT A FREE PRESS

Ensuring the existence of a free press requires the energies and talents of a range of people. There must be reporters who do the job of seeking out information. There must be lawyers who are familiar with the Constitution and the precedents set by the courts. There must be private individuals who consider a candidate's position on freedom of the press when voting. All of these parties are involved in maintaining a free press, but there are also organizations devoted to ensuring a free press.

The American Civil Liberties Union (ACLU) is one such organization. A key issue for the ACLU is censorship. The organization's Web site states, "Censorship is like poison gas: a powerful weapon that can harm you when the wind shifts." In other words, although censorship may not be directed at you or at a cause that you cherish at the moment, it can easily change to affect you. When it does, you will be the one experiencing the harm. Therefore, everyone has an important stake in preventing censorship.

Not all countries have a free press. Tunisian journalists protested for greater freedom in October 2012.

The ACLU's Project on Speech, Privacy, and Technology (SPT) focuses on the impact of new technologies on free speech and privacy rights. The project works on a variety of issues, including political protest, freedom of expression online, privacy of electronic information, and journalists' rights.

The American Press Institute (API) is another organization that is dedicated to the preservation of a free press. Its Web site states, "API advocates the value of newspaper media and all news media, and the value of independent journalism as a cornerstone of democracy." With this in mind, the API offers resources for schools and news outlets. These resources are designed to promote the value of newspapers while helping prepare

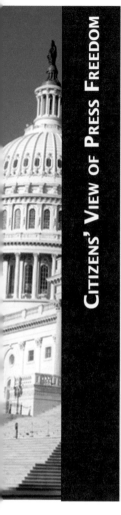

So how do the citizens of the United States view their First Amendment right to a free press? According to *State of the First Amendment: 2012*, a yearly survey conducted by the First Amendment Center, only 13 percent of the people polled were able to name freedom of the press as one of the five specific freedoms in the First Amendment. While they may not think of freedom of the press as part of the First Amendment, 75 percent of people agreed that the news media should act as a government watchdog. However, only about 33 percent believed that the news media attempts to report the news without any bias. When asked for their main source of news about political candidates, 40 percent mentioned television broadcast news, 30 percent named newspapers and their Web sites, and 29 percent named television news organization Web sites.

The *State of the First Amendment* survey indicates that even in our modern society, with an ever-expanding set of news outlets, Americans turn to television broadcast news for information about political candidates. They also continue to view the press as a watchdog—an institution that keeps an eye on government activity and sounds an alarm when the government goes astray.

journalists for greater diversity in the field of news reporting.

# AN EXPANDING FREE PRESS

Traditionally, the free press consisted of newspapers. Today, there are many more outlets for the news. The

Cable and broadcast television networks help inform Americans about political candidates. Above, people gather to watch a presidential debate between Barack Obama and Mitt Romney in 2012.

free press has expanded to include such things as blogs, talk radio, celebrity magazines, and the tabloids.

Blogs, or online journals, are simple to create and maintain—so simple that virtually anyone can have one. Blogs have a variety of purposes. A blog can be a

"Shock jocks" like Howard Stern depend upon free speech protection for their talk radio shows.

place to share recipes or photos, or a place to write one's opinions of the news of the day. A blog can also be used to report news in the community. The right to freedom of speech usually protects what individuals write on a personal blog. The right to freedom of the press may also come into play. The deciding factor is the purpose of the blog. Some blogs are part of a larger Web site with additional information and links to other media, such as videos and podcasts.

Talk radio is just what it sounds like: radio with programming that consists of conversation, not music. Talk radio is not the same as an all-news station. On talk radio, hosts speak, interview, or give advice on topics related to the purpose of the show. The talk-radio host may also report items from the news. Some of the comments made by the host are protected by freedom of speech. If there is a news segment, the content falls under the protections afforded a free press.

Celebrity magazines are magazines that cover the activities of famous people. The people might be movie and television stars, musicians, royalty, prominent businesspeople, or politicians. These publications generally include photos, many of which are taken without the consent of the people photographed. If photographs of a private individual were run without permission, it might be a problem, but celebrity magazines devote their coverage to public figures.

Tabloids are newspapers that contain news that is often sensational in nature. When something reported in a tabloid is untrue, the publication will often be sued. In many instances, celebrities have won their suits with the tabloids. This is significant because public figures have a higher burden of proof to win their suits than private individuals do.

None of these forms of the press existed when the Bill of Rights was written. The Founding Fathers may have had a difficult time imagining such things. Yet they are outlets for the news today and are covered by the protections afforded a free press.

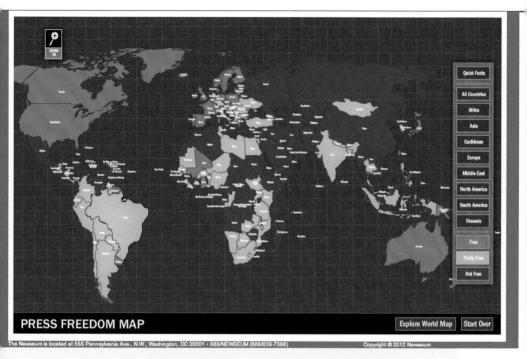

This map from the Newseum evaluates press freedom in countries around the world. Many nations do not enjoy freedom of the press.

# FREEDOM OF THE PRESS IN OTHER COUNTRIES

The Newseum is an interactive museum in Washington, D.C., dedicated to the how and why of news. As one of its exhibits, the museum maintains a map that tracks freedom of the press on a global scale. On the map, countries that are colored green enjoy a free press. Countries in yellow have a press that is partly free, indicating that there is government censorship or other forms of interference from time to time. Countries in red have a press that is not free due to the inability of reporters to cover their stories without censorship, harassment, or other dangers.

The exhibit at the Newseum also includes ratings for each country on a scale of 0 to 100. Higher ratings indicate greater restrictions on the news media. Not surprisingly, democracies are more likely to have a free press than dictatorships or countries with totalitarian forms of government. Countries undergoing a transformation from restrictive governments to freer forms of government may still be listed as lacking a free press, but they may be closer to having a "partly free" press when the individual score is used. Some democracies, such as South Korea, are listed as having a "partly free" press due to the fact that there has been increased government censorship in recent years.

The Newseum uses ratings provided by Freedom House to build its list. Freedom House is an independent private organization that was founded in 1941. Its mission is to support the expansion of democracy and freedom in the world. Each year, Freedom House assigns a score to each country. The score is based upon the level of freedom in that country for print, broadcast, and Internet-based news media. Significantly, the ratings show that the vast majority of people live in countries with media that is "partly free" or "not free." You can view the Newseum's most recent press freedom map at http://www.newseum.org/exhibits -and-theaters/permanent-exhibits/world-news/press -freedom-map.html.

# The Press of the Future

The 2012 Olympic Games in London have often been referred to as the "Twitter Games." This is because so many breaking stories and event results were tweeted as they happened. Many who wished not to know the results of Olympic events until the tapes were aired during U.S. prime time were informed of the results via Twitter.

Twitter is just one of the social media platforms with the capacity to reach a large audience instantaneously. YouTube is another. Anyone can post a video on YouTube. Once it is on the site, anyone can access it. The video can be a record of police activity, an algebra lesson, or coverage of a sporting event. It's no longer the case that a professional reporter or videographer must be the one to capture an event.

CNN also has iReport, a platform that allows individuals to post their stories and footage. And there are many others. All of this adds up to even more opportunities for the news to reach the public from nontraditional sources. Some of these sources did not exist ten years ago, let alone two hundred years ago.

Due to the number of fans and athletes tweeting results and reacting to events at the 2012 Summer Olympics in London, they became known as the "Twitter Games."

## Is This What the Founding Fathers Had in Mind?

The Founding Fathers created a government that would be responsive to the needs of the people. They used their own experience with British rule to make their new government different in ways they hoped would ensure freedom for the people, along with the ability to modify the government as the people saw fit. The government they created had a system of checks and balances to prevent one branch of the government from overpowering the others. It also had a Bill of Rights that listed individual freedoms that the people of the United States

89

could count on. One of those freedoms was freedom of the press.

It has been more than two hundred years since the Bill of Rights was adopted. A free press has existed in the United States for that entire time. The press has grown beyond the traditional newspaper to include a variety of other outlets, including digital outlets. In the future, new forms of media are sure to be introduced. It's just as sure that people will find a way to transmit the news over these new technologies. The net result will be a vibrant and free press that may be very different in appearance from what the Founding Fathers imagined, but just the same in purpose.

# Preamble to the Constitution

*We the People of the United States, in order to form a more perfect Union, establish Justice, insure domestic Tranquility, provide for the common defense, promote the general Welfare, and secure the Blessings of Liberty to ourselves and our Posterity, do ordain and establish this Constitution for the United States of America.*

On September 25, 1789, Congress transmitted to the state legislatures twelve proposed amendments, two of which, having to do with congressional representation and congressional pay, were not adopted. The remaining ten amendments became the Bill of Rights.

# The Bill of Rights

## Amendment I

Congress shall make no law respecting an establishment of religion, or prohibiting the free exercise thereof; or abridging the freedom of speech, or of the press; or the right of the people peaceably to assemble, and to petition the Government for a redress of grievances.

## Amendment II

A well regulated Militia, being necessary to the security of a free State, the right of the people to keep and bear Arms, shall not be infringed.

## Amendment III

No Soldier shall, in time of peace be quartered in any house, without the consent of the Owner, nor in time of war, but in a manner to be prescribed by law.

## Amendment IV

The right of the people to be secure in their persons, houses, papers, and effects, against unreasonable searches and seizures, shall not be violated, and no Warrants shall issue, but upon probable cause, supported by Oath or affirmation, and particularly describing the place to be searched, and the persons or things to be seized.

## Amendment V

No person shall be held to answer for a capital, or otherwise infamous crime, unless on a presentment or indictment of a Grand Jury, except in cases arising in the land or naval forces, or in the Militia, when in actual service in time of War or public danger; nor shall any person be subject for the same offence to be twice put in jeopardy of life or limb; nor shall be

**THE BILL OF RIGHTS**

compelled in any criminal case to be a witness against himself, nor be deprived of life, liberty, or property, without due process of law; nor shall private property be taken for public use, without just compensation.

## Amendment VI

In all criminal prosecutions, the accused shall enjoy the right to a speedy and public trial, by an impartial jury of the State and district wherein the crime shall have been committed, which district shall have been previously ascertained by law, and to be informed of the nature and cause of the accusation; to be confronted with the witnesses against him; to have compulsory process for obtaining witnesses in his favor, and to have the Assistance of Counsel for his defense.

## Amendment VII

In Suits at common law, where the value in controversy shall exceed twenty dollars, the right of trial by jury shall be preserved, and no fact tried by a jury, shall be otherwise re-examined in any Court of the United States, than according to the rules of the common law.

## Amendment VIII

Excessive bail shall not be required, nor excessive fines imposed, nor cruel and unusual punishments inflicted.

THE BILL OF RIGHTS

## Amendment IX

The enumeration in the Constitution, of certain rights, shall not be construed to deny or disparage others retained by the people.

## Amendment X

The powers not delegated to the United States by the Constitution, nor prohibited by it to the States, are reserved to the States respectively, or to the people.

**censorship** The act of keeping something from publication or public distribution because the content is deemed inappropriate or objectionable.

**classified information** Information or material that has been determined by the government to require protection against unauthorized disclosure for reasons of national security.

**Cold War** The period of time after World War II when the United States and its NATO allies, and the Soviet Union and other Communist countries, were engaged in a war of ideas and diplomatic pressures.

**concurring opinion** An opinion that is in agreement with a court's decision in a case but that states different reasons as the basis for the decision.

**dissenting opinion** An opinion that does not agree with a court's decision in a case.

**docket** The cases on a court's calendar.

**elaborate** To work out in detail; develop.

**exempt** Free or released from some requirement.

**exonerate** To free from a charge of guilt.

**journalist** A person who investigates, writes, edits, or reports the news.

**jurisdiction** An area or sphere of authority.

**leak** An intentional disclosure of secret information by an anonymous source.

**libel** A published statement that is false and damaging to a person's reputation.

opinion  A judge's written explanation of a decision of the court or of a majority of the judges.

precedent  A court decision in an earlier case with facts and legal issues similar to a dispute currently before the court.

public figure  In defamation law, an individual who is of great public interest and is widely known.

shield law  A law that protects journalists from being forced to reveal confidential sources.

social media  Technologies that are Internet-based and facilitate the creation and exchange of user-generated content.

subpoena  An order of the court for a person to appear at a particular time and place to testify and/or produce documents in his or her control.

whistleblower  A person, usually an employee in an organization, who reports or informs on a wrongdoer.

**American Civil Liberties Union (ACLU)**
125 Broad Street, 18th Floor
New York, NY 10004
(212) 549-2500
Web site: http://www.aclu.org
The ACLU works to defend the individual rights and freedoms guaranteed in the Constitution and the Bill of Rights, including the First Amendment right to freedom of the press.

**American Society of Journalists and Authors (ASJA)**
1501 Broadway, Suite 403
New York, NY 10036
(212) 997-0947
Web site: http://www.asja.org
The ASJA is devoted to the support and professional development of working journalists and nonfiction writers. The organization has an annual conference and an educational foundation.

**Canadian Civil Liberties Association (CCLA)**
506–360 Bloor Street West
Toronto, ON M5S 1X1
Canada
(416) 363-0321, ext. 225
Web site: http://ccla.org
The CCLA works to reform laws and defend fundamental freedoms in a wide range of public interest and advocacy areas.

**Department of Justice Canada**
284 Wellington Street

Ottawa, ON K1A 0H8
Canada
(613) 957-4222
Web site: http://www.justice.gc.ca
The Department of Justice Canada has programs and initiatives
in place to ensure access to information.

**First Amendment Center at Vanderbilt University**
John Seigenthaler Center
1207 18th Avenue South
Nashville, TN 37212
(615) 727-1600
Web site: http://www.firstamendmentcenter.org
The First Amendment Center is an educational organization concerned with the state of the First Amendment. It has a wide
variety of resources on all aspects of the First Amendment.

**Newseum**
555 Pennsylvania Avenue NW
Washington, DC 20001
(888) NEWSEUM [639-7386]
Web site: http://www.newseum.org
The Newseum is a museum dedicated to the news. Its mission is
to educate the public about the value of a free press in a free
society. Permanent exhibits include the Story of the News,
Pulitzer Prize Photographs, 48 Words of Freedom, and more.

**Supreme Court of the United States**
1 First Street NE
Washington, DC 20543

(202) 479-3000

Web site: http://www.supremecourt.gov
The Web site of the Supreme Court offers information about America's highest court. It provides access to the Court's recent decisions on constitutional issues including freedom of the press.

# WEB SITES

Due to the changing nature of Internet links, Rosen Publishing has developed an online list of Web sites related to the subject of this book. This site is updated regularly. Please use this link to access the list:

http://www.rosenlinks.com/PFCD/Press

Barron, Jerome A., and C. Thomas Dienes. *First Amendment Law in a Nutshell*. 4th ed. St. Paul, MN: Thomson/West, 2008.

Cooke, John Byrne. *Reporting the War: Freedom of the Press from the American Revolution to the War on Terrorism*. New York, NY: Palgrave Macmillan, 2007.

Engdahl, Sylvia. *Blogs* (Current Controversies). Detroit, MI: Greenhaven Press/Gale, 2008.

Epps, Garrett. *The First Amendment: Freedom of the Press: Its Constitutional History and the Contemporary Debate* (Bill of Rights). Amherst, NY: Prometheus Books, 2008.

Gibson, Karen Bush. *John Peter Zenger* (Profiles in American History). Hockessin, DE: Mitchell Lane, 2007.

Gilbert, Sara. *Write Your Own Article: Newspaper, Magazine, Online* (Write Your Own). Mankato, MN: Compass Point Books, 2009.

Hall, Homer L. *Student's Workbook for High School Journalism*. New York, NY: Rosen Publishing Group, 2009.

Harrower, Tim, and Julie M. Elman. *The Newspaper Designer's Handbook*. 7th ed. New York, NY: McGraw-Hill, 2013.

Haynes, Charles C., Sam Chaltain, and Susan M. Glisson. *First Freedoms: A Documentary History* of *First Amendment Rights in America*. New York, NY: Oxford University Press, 2006.

Herda, D. J. *New York Times v. United States: National Security and Censorship* (Landmark Supreme Court Cases). Rev. ed. Berkeley Heights, NJ: Enslow Publishers, 2011.

Jones, Molly. *The First Amendment: Freedom of Speech, the Press, and Religion* (Amendments to the United States Constitution: The Bill of Rights). New York, NY: Rosen Central, 2011.

Lerner, Alicia Cafferty, and Adrienne Wilmoth Lerner. *Freedom of Expression* (Global Viewpoints). Detroit, MI: Greenhaven Press, 2009.

Lewis, Anthony. *Freedom for the Thought That We Hate: A Biography of the First Amendment* (Basic Ideas). New York, NY: Basic Books, 2009.

Lind, Nancy S., and Erik Rankin. *First Amendment Rights: An Encyclopedia*. Santa Barbara, CA: ABC-CLIO, 2013.

Palser, Barb. *Choosing News: What Gets Reported and Why* (Exploring Media Literacy). Mankato, MN: Compass Point Books, 2012.

Patrick, John J. *The Supreme Court of the United States: A Student Companion* (Oxford Student Companions to American Government). 3rd ed. New York, NY: Oxford University Press, 2006.

Robinson, Tom. *The Evolution of News Reporting* (Essential Viewpoints). Edina, MN: ABDO Publishing Company, 2011.

Ruschmann, Paul, and David L. Hudson. *Media Bias* (Point-Counterpoint). 2nd ed. New York, NY: Chelsea House, 2012.

Smith, Rich. *First Amendment: The Right of Expression*. Edina, MN: ABDO Publishing Company, 2008.

Stearman, Kaye. *Freedom of Information* (Ethical Debates). New York, NY: Rosen Central, 2012.

Steven, Peter. *The News* (Groundwork Guides). Berkeley, CA: Groundwood Books, 2010.

Streisel, Jim. *High School Journalism: A Practical Guide*. Jefferson, NC: McFarland & Co., 2007.

Associated Press. "Judges Rebuff Justice Dept. in 3 FOIA Cases." First Amendment Center, March 5, 2012. Retrieved July 20, 2012 (http://www .firstamendmentcenter.org/judges-rebuff-justice -dept-in-3-foia-cases).

Associated Press. "N.Y. Cameraman Files Suit, Claims Police Obstruction." First Amendment Center, April 12, 2012. Retrieved August 1, 2012 (http:// www.firstamendmentcenter.org/n-y-cameraman -files-suit-claims-police-obstruction).

Associated Press. "Top Lawmakers Declare War on Intelligence Leaks." First Amendment Center, June 8, 2012. Retrieved July 20, 2012 (http://www .firstamendmentcenter.org/top-lawmakers-declare -war-on-intelligence-leaks).

Ax, Joseph. "Occupy Protester's Tweets Must Be Handed Over: Judge." *Chicago Tribune*, July 2, 2012. Retrieved July 7, 2012 (http://articles .chicagotribune.com/2012-07-02/news/sns-rt-us -twitter-occupybre86119o-20120702_1_tweets -protester-occupy-related-arrests).

Carter, T. Barton, Marc A. Franklin, and Jay B. Wright. *The First Amendment and the Fifth Estate: Regulation of Electronic Mass Media*. 3rd ed. Westbury, NY: Foundation Press, 1993.

Cook, Timothy E., ed. *Freeing the Presses: The First Amendment in Action*. Baton Rouge, LA: Louisiana State University Press, 2005.

Cornwell, Nancy C. *Freedom of the Press: Rights and Liberties Under the Law*. Santa Barbara, CA: ABC-CLIO, 2004.

Fildes, Jonathan. "What Is WikiLeaks?" BBC News, December 7, 2010. Retrieved August 1, 2012 (http://www.bbc.com/news/technology-10757263).

Friedman, Ian C. *Freedom of Speech and the Press (American Rights)*. New York, NY: Facts On File, 2005.

Hebert, David L. *Freedom of the Press*. Detroit, MI: Greenhaven Press, 2005.

Historical Society of the Courts of the State of New York. "Case and Tryal of John Peter Zenger." Retrieved September 24, 2012 (http://www.courts.state.ny.us/history/elecbook/zenger_tryal/pg1.htm).

Historical Society of the Courts of the State of New York. "The Trial of John Peter Zenger." Retrieved September 24, 2012 (http://www.courts.state.ny.us/history/zenger.htm).

Hornery, Andrew. "Cruise Launches the Lawyers at Divorce Coverage." *Sydney Morning Herald*, July 13, 2012. Retrieved August 2012 (http://www.smh.com.au/lifestyle/celebrity/cruise-launches-the-lawyers-at-divorce-coverage-20120713-220ue.html).

Illinois First Amendment Center. "First Amendment Research Information." 2012. Retrieved September 24, 2012 (http://www.illinoisfirstamendmentcenter.com/research_CourtCases_FreedomOfPress.php).

Illinois First Amendment Center. "The Freedom of the Press." 2012. Retrieved September 24, 2012 (http://www.illinoisfirstamendmentcenter.com/press.php).

Jarrow, Gail. *The Printer's Trial: The Case of John Peter Zenger and the Fight for a Free Press.* Honesdale, PA: Calkins Creek, 2006.

Jennings, Brian. *Censorship: The Threat to Silence Talk Radio.* New York, NY: Threshold Editions, 2009.

Kovach, Bill, and Tom Rosenstiel. *The Elements of Journalism.* New York, NY: Random House, 2003.

Leiter, Richard A., Roy M. Mersky, and Gary R. Hartman. *Landmark Supreme Court Cases: The Most Influential Decisions of the Supreme Court of the United States* (Facts on File Library of American History). 2nd ed. New York, NY: Facts On File, 2012.

Levy, Leonard Williams. *Freedom of the Press from Zenger to Jefferson.* Durham, NC: Carolina Academic Press, 1996.

Lewis, Anthony. *Make No Law: The Sullivan Case and the First Amendment.* New York, NY: Random House, 1991.

McGlone, Catherine. *New York Times v. Sullivan and the Freedom of the Press Debate* (Debating Supreme Court Decisions). Berkeley Heights, NJ: Enslow Publishers, 2005.

Naughton, John. "Web Sites That Changed the World." The *Observer*, August, 12, 2006.

Retrieved August 15, 2012 (http://www.guardian
.co.uk/technology/2006/aug/13/observerreview
.onlinesupplement).

Powe, Lucas A. Scot. *The Fourth Estate and the
Constitution: Freedom of the Press in America.*
Berkeley, CA: University of California Press, 1991.

Rich, Carole, and Christopher Harper. *Writing
and Reporting News: A Coaching Method*
(Wadsworth Series in Mass Communication
and Journalism). 5th ed. Belmont, CA: Thomson
/Wadsworth, 2007.

Ross, Gary. *Who Watches the Watchmen? The
Conflict Between National Security and the
Freedom of the Press* (Foreign Denial &
Deception Series). Washington, DC: National
Intelligence University, Center for Strategic
Intelligence Research, 2011.

Simmons, Amanda. "N.Y. Court Orders Twitter to
Turn Over User Information in Criminal Case."
Reporters Committee for Freedom of the Press,
July 3, 2012. Retrieved July 7, 2012 (http://www
.rcfp.org/browse-media-law-resources/news/ny
-court-orders-twitter-turn-over-user-information
-criminal-case).

Streissguth, Thomas. *Media Bias* (Open for Debate).
New York, NY: Marshall Cavendish Benchmark,
2007.

WikiLeaks.org. "About: What Is WikiLeaks?" Retrieved October 1, 2012 (http://wikileaks.org /About.html).

Willis, Clyde E. *Student's Guide to Landmark Congressional Laws on the First Amendment.* Westport, CT: Greenwood Press, 2002.

## ABOUT THE AUTHOR

Gina Hagler is an award-winning author. She is a member of the Society of Children's Book Writers and Illustrators and the American Society of Journalists and Authors. Hagler writes on a variety of topics for children and adults. She has a special interest in issues surrounding freedom of the press.

## PHOTO CREDITS

Cover, pp. 1, 3, 7, 23, 39, 56, 76 wellphoto/Shutterstock.com; p. 4 Jacob Silberberg/Getty Images; pp. 8–9 Chip Somodevilla/Getty Images; p. 12 Robert Harding Picture Library/SuperStock; p. 16 The New York Public Library/Art Resource, NY; pp. 20–21 Paul J. Richards/AFP/Getty Images; pp. 24, 28–29 Hulton Archive/Getty Images; p. 27 Apic/Hulton Archive/Getty Images; p. 30 Mondadori/Getty Images; pp. 34–35 Ted Thai/Time & Life Pictures/Getty Images; pp. 36–37 Robyn Beck/AFP/GettyImages; pp. 42–43 Mario Tama/Getty Images; p. 45 Joe Raedle/Getty Images; pp. 48–49, 54–55, 72–73, 88–89 © AP Images; pp. 58–59 DOD/Getty Images; pp. 62–63 Chris Wilkins/AFP/Getty Images; pp. 66–67 Leon Neal/AFP/Getty Images; pp. 68–69 Alex Wong/Getty Images; p. 74 Mark Cunningham/Getty Images; pp. 78–79 Fethi Belaid/AFP/GettyImages; pp. 80–81 AFP/GettyImages; pp. 82–83 Getty Images; p. 85 Courtesy Newseum; page and text box border images © iStockphoto.com/Wayne Howard (crowd & flag), © iStockphoto.com/DHuss (U. S. Capitol building), © iStockphoto.com/Andrea Gingerich (faces).

Designer: Les Kanturek; Editor: Andrea Sclarow Paskoff; Photo Researcher: Amy Feinberg